Advice to a Young Disciple

by
John MacArthur, Jr.

MOODY PRESS
CHICAGO

All Scripture quotations, unless noted otherwise, are from the *New
American Standard Bible,* © 1960, 1962, 1963, 1968, 1971, 1972, 1973, 1975,
and 1977 by The Lockman Foundation, and are used by permission.

ISBN: 0-8024-5327-9

1 2 3 4 5 Printing/LC/Year 95 94 93 92 91

Printed in the United States of America

Advice to a Young Disciple

Contents

These Bible studies are taken from messages delivered by Pastor-Teacher John MacArthur, Jr., at Grace Community Church in Sun Valley, California. The recorded messages themselves may be purchased as a series or individually. Please request the current price list by writing to:

"GRACE TO YOU"
P.O. Box 4000
Panorama City, CA 91412

Or call the following toll-free number:
1-800-55-GRACE

1

The Elements of a Strong Spiritual Life— Part 1

Outline

Introduction
A. The Situation Then
B. The Situation Now
C. The Solution Required

Lesson
I. The Exhortation (v. 1)
   A. The Strength Required
   B. The Grace Received
II. The Illustrations (vv. 2-6)
   A. A Teacher (v. 2)
      1. Teachers are part of a process
      2. Teachers are entrusted with the truth
      3. Teachers must be selective
         a) In choosing faithful men
         b) In choosing gifted men

Conclusion
A. Be a Diligent Student of the Truth
B. Clearly Articulate the Truth
C. Be Loyal to the Truth
D. Be Continually Teaching the Truth

Introduction

A. The Situation Then

Timothy was the apostle Paul's son in the faith and a leader in the church at Ephesus. Paul founded that church (Acts 19), but by the time he wrote his second epistle to Timothy the church and its leaders were exhibiting doctrinal error and sinful behavior.

Paul sent Timothy to Ephesus to rectify the problems in that church. First Timothy contains Paul's instructions to Timothy for how to set the Ephesian church in order. Second Timothy was written to encourage Timothy to "be strong" (2 Tim. 2:1) at a time when he was apparently experiencing a lack of resolve in performing his duties.

Second Timothy is the last letter Paul wrote. It was written shortly before he gave his life in the cause of Christ. He wanted to pass the baton of spiritual leadership to Timothy, and he didn't want Timothy to accept it in a weak state. The church was experiencing persecution in Rome, many were refusing to accept the instructions Timothy received from Paul, and Timothy was being confronted by sophisticated philosophical opposition. Paul knew Timothy was young and apparently of timid disposition. In the face of such circumstances he required strength of will.

In 2 Timothy 2:1-7 Paul says, "You therefore, my son, be strong in the grace that is in Christ Jesus. And the things which you have heard from me in the presence of many witnesses, these entrust to faithful men, who will be able to teach others also. Suffer hardship with me, as a good soldier of Christ Jesus. No soldier in active service entangles himself in the affairs of everyday life, so that he may please the one who enlisted him as a soldier. And also if anyone competes as an athlete, he does not win the prize unless he competes according to the rules. The hard-working farmer ought to be the first to receive his share of the crops. Consider what I say, for the Lord will give you understanding in everything."

B. The Situation Now

Several years ago I read a shocking news account of two children who had been discovered in an attic. They had been chained to their beds since birth, and by the time they were discovered they were teenagers. They were malnourished and animalistic in behavior. Their confinement had allowed all the worst traits of human behavior to flourish. As I read that report I thought of the church. In many cases it, too, is malnourished and allows behavior among its members that is more like the animalistic behavior of the world than the righteous standard it has been called to.

During the summer I often travel around the country. Many people say to me, "There aren't any churches in our city where the Word of God is preached with power." They ask me if I know of any good churches in a certain area. Many times I am forced to admit I can't think of any.

Our age seems to have many popular preachers and many popular churches, but few seem to have any power. Though Christianity is popular, the church as a whole is weak. Many Christians seek psychological answers for their personal difficulties because they do not understand their spiritual resources or how to apply them. Some are lured into sin and then try to excuse it. Others are unable to recognize sound doctrine or are unwilling to defend it.

Weak leadership is responsible for the present state of the church. The prophet Hosea said, "Like people, like priests" (Hos. 4:9; NIV*). Weak leaders may produce churches that are active but powerless. In many churches there is talk about Christianity but little conviction, preaching against sin but little confrontation, and doctrinal affirmation but much compromise. Paul's exhortations to Timothy are as needed today as they were in Timothy's day.

New International Version.

C. The Solution Required

My greatest desire is not that I be a popular speaker but a powerful one. I want the strength of God to be evident in my life so that God can use me in a powerful way through His Word and Spirit. That's to be the goal of every Christian. Victory in the Christian life belongs to the strong—not the weak.

Paul affirmed to Timothy the need for strength in the ministry. Timothy was weak and vacillating, and he needed to be reminded to "kindle afresh" the gift that was in him (2 Tim. 1:6). He needed to be reminded that God had not given him "a spirit of timidity, but of power and love and discipline" (v. 7) and that suffering was part of the ministry (v. 8). Timothy had a duty to perform and needed to be reminded of the resources he had in Christ.

Paul's solution to Timothy's problem was to exhort him to be strong. But if Paul had stopped with that advice he would have frustrated Timothy—and us as well. If you're like me, you've probably heard many exhortations to be strong but haven't the faintest idea how to do it. I remember as a child hearing various speakers exhort me to dedication, consecration, and devotedness to Christ, but I never knew what to do. So I'd be like the proverbial man who jumped on a horse and rode off madly in all directions—trying lots of things with little success.

Paul illustrated his exhortation with four different pictures: a teacher, a soldier, an athlete, and a farmer (2 Tim. 2:2-6). They illustrate how we are to be strong in Christ.

Lesson

I. THE EXHORTATION (v. 1)

"You therefore, my son, be strong in the grace that is in Christ Jesus."

"You therefore" points to Paul's previous admonitions to Timothy not to be ashamed (e.g., 1:8, 12, 16). He had just called Timothy to identify with the behavior of Onesiphorus, who had been faithful to Paul during his imprisonment in Rome (1:16-18). Here he issues a command to Timothy to be strong—a command tempered with love.

Paul's words "my son" reflect God's way of dealing with His children. God's commands are given with reminders of His love for us. Timothy was Paul's son in the faith, and Paul had poured his life into Timothy for many years. Paul's exhortation to Timothy reflects the tenderness and love that ought to exist between those in spiritual authority and those they lead.

God is sovereign, yet He requires men in spiritual leadership to preserve, guard, and pass on the truth of the gospel. That responsibility meant that Timothy needed to be reminded of his spiritual resources and encouraged to be strong in the face of his responsibilities.

A. The Strength Required

Timothy was to "be strong" (v. 1). Paul uses the Greek verb *endunamoō*, which is stated as a present passive imperative and could be translated, "Keep on being empowered." The connotation is similar to that of Ephesians 6:10: "Be strong in the Lord, and in the strength of His might." Timothy was not to be strong in his own strength but in God's. He was to receive God's power and allow it to flow through him.

Jude 21 says, "Keep yourselves in the love of God." Jude meant that his readers were to keep themselves in the place where God's love and blessing could be received. We do that by being obedient to Him and taking advantage of the means of grace available to us—the study of God's Word, prayer, fasting, and meditation. That's how we position ourselves to receive His power.

B. The Grace Received

Perhaps the best translation of 2 Timothy 2:1 is, "Be strong by means of the grace that is in Christ Jesus."

Believers exist in the sphere of grace through our union with Christ. It's the grace of God that empowers believers.

We are saved by grace through faith (Eph. 2:8). Grace is the undeserved favor of God extended through the gift of salvation—it can't be earned. Once grace is extended to us it's always ours. That's important because if God withdrew His grace, our present sins would condemn us. By living in the sphere of grace we are continually cleansed of our sins (1 John 1:9).

God's grace extends to us not only forgiveness but also divine power. Romans 5:2 speaks of "this grace in which we stand." The Greek word translated "stand" (*histēmi*) means "to be fixed." It is by God's grace that we are both forgiven and have the power to stand in the sphere of grace.

It's God's grace that enables us to serve God—otherwise we could do nothing. God's will is accomplished "'not by might nor by power, but by My Spirit,' says the Lord of hosts" (Zech. 4:6). That's the kind of grace Paul is speaking of in 2 Timothy 2:1.

II. THE ILLUSTRATIONS (vv. 2-6)

Paul drew four pictures to help Timothy understand how to "be strong in the grace that is in Christ Jesus" (v. 1). Like the parabolic teachings of Christ, they serve as vivid illustrations of spiritual truth.

A. A Teacher (v. 2)

"The things which you have heard from me in the presence of many witnesses, these entrust to faithful men, who will be able to teach others also."

Paul wanted Timothy to view himself as a teacher. Verse 2 pictures teachers teaching prospective teachers. Paul wanted Timothy to pass on what he had learned to "faithful men" who would become teachers. They in turn would teach others, and the line of teaching would continue.

The True Apostolic Succession

The true apostolic succession was not of office but of doctrine. Jesus taught the twelve apostles, they taught the next generation of teachers, and that chain of doctrinal truth has continued down to today. Christians are part of a living chain of doctrinal truth that reaches back to Christ Himself. In Acts 1:1 Luke writes that the first account he composed (the gospel of Luke) was "about all that Jesus *began* to do and teach" (emphasis added). Though He finished the work of redemption, Jesus only began the work of teaching and preaching the truth of the gospel. That work must continue as an indestructible chain.

An Unbroken Chain

At home I have a portrait of my great-grandfather in his ecclesiastical robes. That's what he wore when he preached God's Word in Scotland. My grandfather was also a preacher, as was my father, who preached God's Word to me. So to me that painting portrays the chain that stretches all the way back to Jesus Christ. The chain is unbroken because it represents the teaching of Christ preserved in the Word of God that's been passed all the way down to you and me.

1. Teachers are part of a process

   In verse 2 Paul reminds Timothy that he is part of a process. I remember participating in a mile relay race while in college. Our first runner ran a great leg and passed the baton to me. I ran as hard as I could, and when I handed the baton to the third man, we were tied for first place. We thought we could win because both our third and fourth runners were especially fast. After receiving the baton our third man started running around the curve, down the back stretch—and then stopped. He walked off the track and sat down.

   We all thought he had injured himself and ran over to find out what happened. I'll never forget his reply when we asked what was wrong: "I don't know—I just don't feel like running today." We couldn't believe

13

it! Like Timothy, that runner was a part of a process. He didn't have the right to stop when others were counting on him and striving with him. Paul didn't want Timothy to be the broken link in the chain of preaching the gospel of Christ.

2. Teachers are entrusted with the truth

The phrase "the things which you have heard from me" refers to the doctrine Paul had taught Timothy. Paul had entrusted Timothy with revelation from God. He expected Timothy to entrust that same teaching to others.

The verb translated "entrust" (Gk., *paratithēmi*) means "to deposit for safekeeping." Paul was referring to the deposit of revelation he had left with Timothy. He spoke of the same thing elsewhere.

a) 2 Timothy 1:12-14—"I know whom I have believed and I am convinced that He is able to guard what I have entrusted to Him until that day. Retain the standard of sound words which you have heard from me, in the faith and love which are in Christ Jesus. Guard, through the Holy Spirit who dwells in us, the treasure which has been entrusted to you." Paul had entrusted his life to God. Timothy was to guard what had been entrusted to him—God's Word.

b) 1 Timothy 6:20—"Guard what has been entrusted to you, avoiding worldly and empty chatter and the opposing arguments of what is falsely called 'knowledge.'" Guarding the "sound words" (2 Tim. 1:13) of God meant avoiding empty words.

A better translation of the phrase "in the presence of many witnesses" (2 Tim. 2:2) is "supported by the confirming testimony of many witnesses." Paul wasn't referring to an ordination ceremony where Timothy was given a particular charge in the presence of many. Rather, Paul wanted Timothy to remember that the revelation he received from Paul had been confirmed by many witnesses to be of divine origin. Paul was often accompanied by many teachers (e.g., Acts 20:4), and he was one of five who ministered at Antioch (Acts 13:1). The apostle Peter attested that Paul's writings were Scripture (2 Pet. 3:15-16).

In addition to the importance of guarding the truth is the responsibility every spiritual leader has to give it away. He needs to guard its purity and pass it on to others in that pure form. "These" in 2 Timothy 2:2 refers to the truth entrusted to Timothy that he was to "entrust to faithful men."

The Primary Role of a Man of God

The primary role of a man of God is to maintain the purity of the Word and pass it on to the next generation intact. That's the reason The Master's Seminary was formed. I believe I must do all I can to raise up godly leadership for the next generation of the church. If the church is weak, it's because of weak leaders. The goal of the seminary is to build strong leaders to build a strong church. I can't rely on others to do that job—it's my responsibility as much as anyone's. That's also the reason for The Master's College. I hope those two institutions will produce generations of people who hold to the truth of God in its purity. They exist as two means of guarding the truth entrusted to us as believers.

Romans 3:2 says a chief advantage the Jewish people had was being "entrusted with the oracles of God." Timothy had also been entrusted with revelation, and it was essential that he pass it on so he could join Paul in Rome for the apostle's final hours (cf. 2 Tim. 4:9). I have a compulsion to pass on what had been entrusted to me. That's why I write books and commentaries on the Bible. All the ministries I am involved in—whether preaching or generating tapes and a radio broadcast—are geared toward my primary role of passing on the truth in its purity to the next generation.

3. Teachers must be selective

The truth is to be passed on to "faithful men . . . able to teach others also" (2 Tim. 2:2). Later Paul instructed Timothy to "preach the word" (2 Tim. 4:2) in a general sense to all, but here Paul is concerned that Timothy be selective in training future preachers and teachers.

I can relate to that. During the many years of my ministry I've concentrated on two priorities: preaching the Word to all and building godly leaders. Building godly leaders requires that I be selective—you can't minister to everyone on a one-on-one basis. So I seek to find men I can invest my life in.

a) In choosing faithful men

Verse 2 says those men are to be faithful men—men of proved spiritual character. The Greek word translated "faithful" is translated "trustworthy" in verse 11. If I am going to invest my life in a man, I don't want him to turn out like Phygelus, Hermogenes, or Demas (2 Tim. 1:15; 4:10)—men who would forsake me because of love for the world. The kind of men I want to spend my life discipling are loyal to the Word of God and dedicated to preserving its truth.

Many spend large amounts of time with problem-plagued people who aren't faithful. Certainly such people need much love and tenderness, but unless they become faithful, they will never make a difference for Christ. Although I do not want to be insensitive to others, I do want to pour myself into those who will make a difference—those who will be faithful to guard and articulate the truth.

b) In choosing gifted men

Verse 2 indicates that the men I should invest my time in are those "who will be able to teach others also." Paul wanted Timothy to be a teacher-maker, and that's what I want to be. Beyond the issue of character is the issue of giftedness. I have the gift of teaching, and it's that gift I seek to develop in others who have it.

I remember after counseling a man in our church several times he told me, "I don't know if this helps you or not, but I don't think you have the gift of counseling." I took that as an opportunity to focus myself. I don't try to teach others how to do things I can't do. Instead I try to teach and encourage others who have gifts similar to my own, which is what God wants us all to do.

Conclusion

Every pastor is to model what those in the church are to be. That means pastors are to model what it means to preserve and pass on the truth of the gospel. That's because every Christian is to be part of that process—perhaps at different levels and in different ways but with the same goal. Peter said to "always . . . be prepared to give an answer to everyone who asks you to give the reason for the hope that you have" (1 Pet. 3:15, NIV). Each of us is to be diligent to present himself "approved to God as a workman who does not need to be ashamed, handling accurately the word of truth" (2 Tim. 2:15).

First Timothy 5:17 says, "Let the elders who rule well be considered worthy of double honor, especially those who work hard at preaching and teaching." The Lord honors those who are faithful to guard the truth and pass it on in its purity. We need to be part of the process of teaching wherever we are—either by teaching or being taught.

Why Teach?

We retain what we teach. When I read a book without doing anything with its contents, I generally forget what it's about. But when I take its principles and teach them to others, I never forget it. We all ought to learn to teach. Husbands ought to teach their wives, and wives can teach their husbands; if you've learned spiritual truth during the day, tell each other! Parents ought to teach their children, and children who are learning God's Word ought to share it with their parents, friends, and classmates. We can all share spiritual truth at work and with fellow believers in times of prayer and study. When you write letters, tell what you have been learning. Get a group of young people or young Christians together and teach them.

The point is this: pass on God's truth in its pure form to the next generation. Our world is falling apart morally and spiritually, and God's Word is the only measure of reality. To pass on the truth successfully we must be committed to knowing it and teaching it to others.

Anyone who wants to be a strong believer must see himself as a teacher. That means being willing to do a number of things.

A. Be a Diligent Student of the Truth

If you want to be a teacher you must first diligently study what you will teach (2 Tim. 2:15).

B. Clearly Articulate the Truth

A teacher of the truth must be clear. That's necessary for others to understand your hope in Christ (1 Pet. 3:15) and "the things which are fitting for sound doctrine" (Titus 2:1).

C. Be Loyal to the Truth

A teacher of the truth must be loyal to it. If you want to be blessed and empowered by God, you must live in accordance with His Word. A teacher is willing to fight for the truth, and that presupposes living by it. Once truth is part of your life, fighting for it is natural.

D. Be Continually Teaching the Truth

Teachers of the truth must continually be involved in the process of equipping others. As in a relay race, those who teach God's Word must be prepared to receive, run with, and pass on the baton of the pure truth of God.

Our Lord wants strong believers who are empowered by Him. That means being a teacher entrusted with the truth and faithful to pass it on.

Focusing on the Facts

1. When Paul wrote his second epistle to Timothy, what characterized the church in Ephesus and its leaders (see p. 8)?
2. Why did Paul send Timothy to Ephesus? What did he write about in his two letters to Timothy (see p. 8)?
3. Describe what characterizes the church in our age. What is responsible for that situation (see p. 9)?
4. What was Paul's solution to Timothy's problem? What illustrations did he use (see p. 10)?
5. What did Timothy's responsibilities require that he be reminded of (see p. 11)?
6. What does the Greek verb translated "be strong" in 2 Timothy 2:2 imply about the source of our strength (see p. 11)?
7. How does God's grace operate in the lives of believers (see p. 12)?
8. How did Paul want Timothy to view himself (see p. 12)?
9. Explain the true apostolic succession (see p. 13).
10. What does the Greek verb translated "entrust" literally mean? What had Timothy been entrusted with? What was he expected to do with it (see p. 14)?
11. How might the phrase "in the presence of many witnesses" be better translated? Why (see pp. 14-15)?
12. In what sense are teachers in the church to be selective? Describe the character and ability teachers are to choose (see p. 16).
13. What are we all to do with our gifts (see p. 17)?
14. Describe the different ways we can teach those we regularly come into contact with (see pp. 17-18).
15. Summarize what a teacher in the church must be willing to do (see p. 18).

Pondering the Principles

1. One wonders whether Timothy had forgotten the meaning of grace, judging from Paul's exhortation in 2 Timothy 2:1—something we are all prone to do. At times does it seem you have no power and are faced with overwhelming problems? Do you ever feel as if God's grace has been withdrawn from your life? Puritan Thomas Goodwin observed that God's grace is "absolute, unchangeable, irreversible, where it is once pitched. If I in seeking God can find this grace of God to own me and embrace me while I seek it, then what do I come to? To a state of irreversible grace, of grace that will carry on the work, that will undertake all for me, that is faithful, and will do it" (*The Works of Thomas Goodwin*, vol. 8 [Edinburgh: The Banner of Truth Trust, 1985 reprint], p. 197). Christians can take comfort that God has extended His grace to us and that "neither death, nor life, nor angels, nor principalities, nor things present, nor things to come, nor powers, nor height, nor depth, nor any other created thing, shall be able to separate us from the love of God, which is in Christ Jesus our Lord" (Rom. 8:38-39).

2. The process of teaching can be likened to the relationship between a shepherd and his sheep: the shepherd is responsible to feed and the sheep must have food. American pastor Charles Jefferson wrote, "When the minister goes into the pulpit, he is the shepherd in the act of feeding, and if every minister had borne this in mind, many a sermon would have been other than it has been. The curse of the pulpit is the superstition that a sermon is a work of art and not a piece of bread or meat" (*The Minister as Shepherd* [Hong Kong: Living Books for All, 1973], p. 61). Is whatever teaching you do—your study, preparation, and speaking—done wholly with the spiritual hunger of God's sheep in mind?

2

The Elements of a Strong Spiritual Life— Part 2

Outline

Introduction
A. The Promise of Empowerment
B. The Reminder About Our Resources

Review
I. The Exhortation (v. 1)
II. The Illustrations (vv. 2-6)
A. A Teacher (v. 2)

Lesson
B. A Soldier (vv. 3-4)
1. He knows he's at war
2. He knows he must suffer hardship
3. He knows he's on active duty
4. He knows he must avoid entanglements
5. He seeks to please his commander
C. An Athlete (v. 5)
1. He must expend maximum effort
2. He must have a goal
3. He must be self-sacrificing
4. He must abide by the rules
5. He must be self-disciplined

D. A Farmer (v. 6)
   1. He must endure hard work
   2. He reaps great blessings
III. The Understanding (v. 7)

Conclusion

Introduction

A. The Promise of Empowerment

   1. Acts 1:8—Jesus said to His disciples, "You shall receive power when the Holy Spirit has come upon you."

   2. Luke 24:49—He promised, "You [will be] clothed with power from on high."

   3. Ephesians 3:20—God "is able to do exceeding abundantly beyond all that we ask or think, according to the power that works within us."

B. The Reminder About Our Resources

   When we forget our spiritual resources and rely on our own strength, we experience discouragement, weariness, and disillusionment. Spiritual warfare is difficult, and it never stops. Timothy, like us, needed to be reminded of his source of spiritual strength. Scripture records many such reminders.

   1. Joshua 1:6-7—God said to Joshua, "Be strong and courageous, for you shall give this people possession of the land which I swore to their fathers to give them. Only be strong and very courageous; be careful to do according to all the law which Moses My servant commanded you; do not turn from it to the right or to the left, so that you may have success wherever you go."

   2. 1 Chronicles 22:13—David said to his son Solomon, "You shall prosper, if you are careful to observe the

statutes and the ordinances which the Lord commanded Moses concerning Israel. Be strong and courageous, do not fear nor be dismayed."

3. 1 Corinthians 16:13—Paul exhorted the Corinthians to "be on the alert, stand firm in the faith, act like men, be strong."

4. Galatians 4:19—Paul spoke to the Galatians as those "with whom I am again in labor until Christ is formed in you." He wanted them to be fully like Christ: strong, mature, and powerful (cf. Eph. 4:13).

5. Colossians 1:28—Paul proclaimed Christ, "admonishing every man and teaching every man with all wisdom, that we may present every man complete in Christ." To be complete in Christ is to be strong spiritually.

6. Ephesians 6:10—Believers are to "be strong in the Lord, and in the strength of His might."

Review

I. THE EXHORTATION (v. 1; see pp. 10-12)

"You therefore, my son, be strong in the grace that is in Christ Jesus."

II. THE ILLUSTRATIONS (vv. 2-6)

A. A Teacher (v. 2; see pp. 12-17)

"The things which you have heard from me in the presence of many witnesses, these entrust to faithful men, who will be able to teach others also."

Lesson

The next three illustrations are a series of metaphors.

B. A Soldier (vv. 3-4)

"Suffer hardship with me, as a good soldier of Christ Jesus. No soldier in active service entangles himself in the affairs of everyday life, so that he may please the one who enlisted him as a soldier."

1. He knows he's at war

Paul likened the Christian to a soldier. That implies we are at war—a metaphor used elsewhere in Scripture.

a) Ephesians 6:11-12—"Put on the full armor of God, that you may be able to stand firm against the schemes of the devil. For our struggle is not against flesh and blood, but against the rulers, against the powers, against the world forces of this darkness, against the spiritual forces of wickedness in the heavenly places."

b) 2 Corinthians 10:3-5—"Though we walk in the flesh, we do not war according to the flesh, for the weapons of our warfare are not of the flesh, but divinely powerful for the destruction of fortresses. We are destroying speculations and every lofty thing raised up against the knowledge of God, and we are taking every thought captive to the obedience of Christ."

Second Timothy 2:3 says we are to be "good" (Gk., *kalos*) soldiers. We are not to be soldiers simply in terms of function and duty—we are to be excellent, noble, and heroic soldiers. That is the kind of soldier who earns medals of valor and honor.

The Real War

It's often hard for Christians in the United States to remember we are at war. We live in a society that, while philosophically hostile to Christianity, has not been hostile legally or politically. That's unlike other countries in the world where the battle lines are more clearly drawn. Elsewhere Christians have often been required to make extreme sacrifices in every area of life. Heroism for Christ's cause is not thrust upon us, so it is easy to forget we are warriors. Though our warfare may not seem evident, the battle is all around us.

- Against Demons

  I will never forget a battle with a demon-possessed girl one night at church. She was in one of the rooms of the church kicking, screaming, and throwing around furniture. When I walked into the room, she said, "Don't let him in!" But the voice that spoke wasn't her own. My first response was, "Fine, I'm leaving!" But I realized that if the demons didn't like me, it was because I was on God's side. I entered, and the girl attacked me, kicking me in the shins so violently that I began to bleed. In the power of God several of us spent hours there until she confessed her sin and God, in His grace purified her. As I left that night I realized for the first time the extent of our warfare against demons.

- Against Unbelief

  A number of years ago a UCLA philosophy professor who was Jewish expressed a desire to know Christ. I presented the gospel to him and met with him early in the morning for six months. After that time he told me he didn't want to meet with me anymore. He went on to attend a liberal seminary and became an Episcopalian rector. I don't know his present spiritual state—but he's not where I intended him to be. Our warfare is for the hearts, minds, and souls of people. It's often most evident in our discipling relationships because that's where unbelief becomes most evident.

- Against Sin

  I have retrieved wayward husbands from places they should not have been. Our church has experienced lawsuits, threats, and accusations. Such experiences affirm that Christians are at war against sin.

First Thessalonians 4:11 says "to make it your ambition to lead a quiet life and attend to your own business." There are quiet times in the Christian life, but they seem to be the exception rather than the rule. They give us time to catch our breath before the next wave hits, for the battle continues to rage.

2. He knows he must suffer hardship

In 2 Timothy 2:3 the Greek word translated "suffer hardship with" (*sunkakopathēson*) could also be translated "endure affliction together," "take your share of suffering," or "take your share of rough treatment." Too often Christianity is presented to nonbelievers as the cure-all to their anxieties, difficulties, and trials. That results in a lot of false disciples. Too few present the gospel by saying, "Come to Christ, pick up your armor, and join us in a lifelong struggle against the world, the flesh, and the devil."

3. He knows he's on active duty

Christians are "in active service" (v. 4). The Christian army does not have any members on rest and recreation. All are on the front lines of an active battle. We all suffer together.

Some think they can be Christians but not fight as Christian soldiers. They're only deceiving themselves —we're on the front line. Such Christians are asleep on the firing line—a dangerous position to be in.

4. He knows he must avoid entanglements

The Greek word translated "entangles" (Gk., *emplekō*) in verse 4 means "to interweave." A believer's life is not to be wrapped up in the nonessentials of this life. Because we live on the battlefront, all things are to be secondary to winning the battle.

Luke 9 gives three examples of people entangled in the things of this life and who thus could not follow our Lord. One was concerned about his personal comfort (vv. 57-58). Another wanted his inheritance first (vv. 59-60). The third was unwilling to give himself wholeheartedly to Jesus as Lord (vv. 61-62). Their lives were interweaved with nonessentials.

No Time-Outs

A soldier on active duty is always a soldier. He can't call a "time-out" in the middle of battle. The same is true of Christians. Like soldiers in the field, we must avoid anything that would hamper us in battle. We're to be so consumed with our duties that though the enticements of the world pass by, we are oblivious to them.

5. He seeks to please his commander

A soldier desires to "please the one who enlisted him as a soldier" (2 Tim. 2:4). That refers to a soldier's commander. A Christian's commander is Jesus Christ. That's whom we endeavor to please.

Christian soldiers are to serve the Lord "with all humility" (Acts 20:19). With that kind of attitude, each of us should be able to say, "I do not consider my life of any account as dear to myself, in order that I may finish my course, and the ministry which I received from the Lord Jesus" (v. 24). Our Lord is the preeminent example of one about whom the Father could say, "[With Him] I am well pleased" (Matt. 3:17). The greatest joy of a Christian will be to hear, "Well done, good and faithful soldier" (cf. Matt. 25:21, 23). Our instinctive response to our Lord ought to be respect and obedience from the heart.

C. An Athlete (v. 5)

"If anyone competes as an athlete, he does not win the prize unless he competes according to the rules."

An athlete is Paul's second metaphor showing how to be strong in the grace of Christ. Paul often made use of athletic metaphors (e.g., 1 Cor. 9:24-26; Eph. 6:12). In 2 Timothy 2:5 Paul uses the Greek verb *athleō* to speak of those who participate in athletic contests.

1. He must expend maximum effort

   Athletes must expend effort. Although athletic contests are often determined by talent, they are *always* determined by effort. That expenditure of effort must begin with a time of preparation long before the contest begins.

2. He must have a goal

   An athlete wants to win a prize. No one watches a basketball game just to see his team dribble a basketball around in circles. Neither will someone run just to hear people applaud his or her performance in a race that has no finish line. We understand that contests require winners.

3. He must be self-sacrificing

   For maximum effort an athlete must be self-sacrificing. You may have seen a race where the runner came across the finish line at the peak of his speed and then collapsed, having totally exhausted his physical resources. That's the kind of effort we are to expend in our Christian lives.

4. He must abide by the rules

   A runner who hopes to obtain the "prize" (v. 5; Gk., *stephanos*, "the winner's crown") must compete according to the rules. In the Olympic games every athlete had to meet three prerequisites: he had to be a true-born Greek, he had to prepare for ten months before the games and affirm that he had done so before a statue of Zeus (he gave Zeus liberty to take his life if he lied), and he had to abide by the rules of his event. If he failed to meet any of those requirements, he was immediately disqualified (Paul speaks of such disqualification in 1 Cor. 9:27). Similarly, believers must be truly born of God, fully trained spiritually, and willing to abide by the rules to be spiritually victorious.

5. He must be self-disciplined

Victory belongs to the disciplined. Most Christians never use the gifts God has given them to their full potential because they never learn to discipline themselves. Self-discipline is a mark of spiritual maturity. The self-disciplined have learned to control their affections, emotions, and priorities. That means refusing to do anything that will dull your competitive edge or sap your spiritual strength.

D. A Farmer (v. 6)

"The hard-working farmer ought to be the first to receive his share of the crops."

Paul's third metaphor is a hardworking farmer—one who tills the ground, working to the point of exhaustion. It's a picture in marked contrast to the previous three.

1. He must endure hard work

A teacher has the joy of watching his students learn and grow. A soldier experiences the thrill of victory. An athlete enjoys the moment of reward. But a farmer's lot is the perpetual duty of the seasons. He plows, sows, tends, and reaps. Whether early or late, sun or snow, heat or cold, he must carry on with his duties. He fights too much water, too little water, bugs, and weeds. He waits patiently to see his crop mature, but when and if a harvest is brought in, the satisfaction of a successful harvest is overshadowed by the prospect of beginning the process all over again.

I understand the point Paul made. I have known the thrills of the ministry as a teacher, soldier, and athlete. But much of the ministry is routine: you plow, sow, tend, reap, wait, and hope. That requires a willingness to work hard without thrills.

Many today are reluctant to work hard in the ministry. I often tell young men that if they desire a successful ministry, they need to be committed to working to exhaustion—often without any encouragement from others. Even with that kind of commitment, the crop often does not come in as expected.

2. He reaps great blessings

There's hard work, but verse 6 also makes the point that when the crop does come in the farmer ought to receive the first of the harvest. Many blessings await those who work hard in ministry—both in the present and in the future. Few work themselves to the point of exhaustion, but only they will experience the blessings Paul speaks of here. *Great reward from God comes only from great labor for God.* In the future it will be the privilege of all hardworking servants of Christ to throw their great rewards at the feet of their Savior.

III. THE UNDERSTANDING (v. 7)

"Consider what I say, for the Lord will give you understanding in everything."

Each of Paul's illustrations requires a degree of self-denial. That means enduring suffering, discipline, or exhaustion. It requires that we avoid entanglement in the things of the world and obey God's rules. Yet our Lord promises a present harvest and future victory.

The Greek word translated "consider" (*noeō*) means "to think over," "ponder," or "understand." It's an unusual command in the New Testament. Paul wanted Timothy to pause in his reading and ponder what he had been told. Did his life reflect the character indicated by Paul's illustrations? That's the same question we must ask ourselves.

With that kind of pondering comes the promise that "the Lord will give you understanding in everything." If we have the spiritual integrity to examine our lives, God will show us where we are in our spiritual walk. The psalmist said to God, "Give me understanding, that I may learn Thy commandments" (Ps. 119:73). That's the kind of understanding we must have.

Conclusion

A common thread running through Paul's illustrations is the promise of reward that comes from hard work. A teacher has his prize students, a soldier his victory in battle, an athlete his victor's crown, and a farmer his harvest. That's the promise of Hebrews 6:10: "God is not unjust so as to forget your work and the love which you have shown toward His name, in having ministered and in still ministering to the saints." Our Lord has promised to give abundantly to those who give abundantly to Him!

Focusing on the Facts

1. What passages in Scripture affirm that Christians are empowered (see p. 22)?
2. What passages in Scripture remind us of our source of spiritual strength? What kind of exhortations do they contain (see pp. 22-23)?
3. The three illustrations found in 2 Timothy 2:3-6 are a series of _____ (see p. 24).
4. Paul's likening a Christian to a soldier implies that we are _____ (see p. 24).
5. Christians are not soldiers only in terms of function and duty. What kind of soldiers are we to be (see p. 24)?
6. Why is it often hard for Christians in the United States to remember we are at war (see p. 25)?
7. Quiet times give Christians time to catch our breath before the next wave of _____ _____ (see p. 26).
8. What happens when Christianity is presented to nonbelievers as the cure to all anxieties, difficulties, and trials (see p. 26)?
9. Because we live on the battlefront, all things are to be _____ to winning the battle (see p. 26).
10. In what Scripture passages other than 2 Timothy 2:3-6 does Paul use the metaphor of an athlete? What kinds of athletes does Paul describe in those passages (see p. 28)?

11. When must the effort of an athlete start (see p. 28)?

12. Describe the rules of the Greek games. How are those rules similar to the rules a Christian is to abide by (see pp. 28-29)?

13. Why do most Christians never use the gifts God has given them to their full potential (see p. 29)?

14. How does Paul's picture of the farmer differ from his preceding three metaphors (see p. 29)?

15. Blessings await those who _____ _____ in ministry (see p. 30).

16. What question must we, like Timothy, ask ourselves (see p. 30)?

17. A common thread running through Paul's illustrations is the promise of _____ (see p. 31).

Pondering the Principles

1. It's natural for a soldier to seek to please his commander, an athlete to discipline himself, and a hardworking farmer to enjoy the fruits of his labor. Similarly, "as there is no law to compel the body to eat or drink, to digest, to sleep . . . or to do the works of nature, for it is ready to do them of itself when the case so requireth, without respect of reward or punishment . . . even so, after the same sort altogether, doth the godly man behave concerning the works of godliness. He is carried to the doing of them by his new nature, which is of the Spirit" (Daniel Cawdray, cited in *The Golden Treasury of Puritan Quotations*, ed. I. D. E. Thomas [Edinburgh: Banner of Truth Trust, 1977], p. 51). Is your life centered on Christ and your activities on doing godly works?

2. Too often the gospel message today is reduced to accepting Christ rather than enlisting to serve Christ. American pastor A. W. Tozer said, "The trouble is that the 'Accept Christ' attitude is likely to be wrong. It shows Christ applying to us rather than us to Him. It makes Him stand hat-in-hand awaiting our verdict on Him, instead of our kneeling with troubled hearts awaiting His verdict on us. It may even permit us to accept Christ by an impulse of mind or emotions, painlessly, at no loss to our ego and no inconvenience to our way of life" (cited in *Signposts: A Collection of Sayings from A. W. Tozer* [Wheaton, Ill.: Victor, 1988], p. 24). How do

you present Christ to others—as a beggar who would like to serve us or as the exalted Lord of the universe who has the right of service from every creature?

3

Motives for Sacrificial Ministry— Part 1

Outline

Introduction
A. The Necessity of Sacrifice
B. The Extremity of Sacrifice

Lesson
I. The Preeminence of Christ (v. 8)
A. His Deity
B. His Humanity and Royalty
C. His Suffering
D. His Example
E. His Resurrection
F. His Worthy Cause
II. The Power of the Word (v. 9)
A. The Bound Messenger
    1. Paul's imprisonment
    2. Paul's critics
B. The Unbound Message
    1. The testimony of Martin Luther
    2. The testimony of the early church
    3. The testimony of John Bunyan
    4. The testimony of the church in China

Conclusion

Introduction

Second Timothy 2:8-13 says, "Remember Jesus Christ, risen from the dead, descendant of David, according to my gospel, for which I suffer hardship even to imprisonment as a criminal; but the word of God is not imprisoned. For this reason I endure all things for the sake of those who are chosen, that they also may obtain the salvation which is in Christ Jesus and with it eternal glory. It is a trustworthy statement: For if we died with Him, we shall also live with Him; if we endure, we shall also reign with Him; if we deny Him, He also will deny us; if we are faithless, He remains faithful; for He cannot deny Himself."

Second Timothy is a call to continue courageously in service to Jesus Christ. Timothy was in a difficult situation and was apparently not fulfilling all his responsibilities. In verses 8-13 Paul gives motivations for sacrificial service that all Christians can learn from.

A. The Necessity of Sacrifice

Jesus made clear that to confess Him as Lord means to submit to Him and serve His cause.

1. John 14:15—"If you love Me, you will keep My commandments." That often involves sacrifice and suffering.

2. Luke 9:23—"If anyone wishes to come after Me, let him deny himself, and take up his cross daily, and follow Me." The Christian is to obey Christ even if it costs him his life.

3. John 15:20—"Remember the word that I said to you, 'A slave is not greater than his master.' If they persecuted Me, they will also persecute you; if they kept My word, they will keep yours also."

4. Matthew 10:17-18—"Beware of men; for they will deliver you up to the courts, and scourge you in their synagogues; and you shall even be brought before governors and kings for My sake, as a testimony to them and to the Gentiles."

Hebrews 11 contains a list of great Old Testament heroes who gave their lives for the Messiah yet to come. We are to give our lives for the Messiah who has already come and whom we know personally.

B. The Extremity of Sacrifice

A believer may be called to make the supreme sacrifice of death. Allegiance to Christ necessarily requires that he or she give up personal desires and ambitions. Those ideas are hard for us in the United States to relate to—we live in a religiously comfortable environment. But whereas the example of the millions who have died for their faith in Christ in other times and parts of the world has apparently had little impact on us, we can relate to a husband or wife deserted by a spouse because of opposition to Christ. That can be worse than death because at least death ushers a believer into the presence of Christ.

Persecution may take many forms, but we may be sure that the Word of God and a godly life will create conflict with the world. As 2 Timothy 3:12 says, "All who desire to live godly in Christ Jesus will be persecuted." Second Timothy 2:8-13 presents the reasons that make that suffering worthwhile. Like Timothy, we are to understand that our service to Christ is worth far more than any personal considerations.

Second Timothy was the last letter Paul wrote. It was a passing of the baton—Paul wanted Timothy to pick up and carry on where Paul would soon be leaving off. He wanted Timothy to be willing to make the same sacrifices he had made for Christ.

Persecution by a Mad Emperor

Timothy lived at a time of increasing pagan hostility toward the church. It's possible he anticipated bodily harm to himself or even death because of it.

The first major persecution of the church was brought on by the burning of Rome in July A.D. 64. Rome burned for six days, and many public buildings were destroyed. Vast areas of tenement buildings were also destroyed, and as a result much of the populace lost their homes.

As Rome burned, the Emperor Nero stood in a tower and watched. It is said he was thrilled at what he called "the beauty of the flames" (Suetonius, *The Twelve Caesars*). It soon became apparent that Nero himself was responsible for the conflagration—he wanted to destroy old Rome so that he could build a new and more magnificent one.

The population turned against him. According to first-century Roman historian Tacitus, "All human efforts, all the lavish gifts of the emperor and propitiations of the gods did not banish the sinister belief that the conflagration was the result of an order [by Nero]. Consequently, to get rid of the report, Nero fastened the guilt and inflicted the utmost tortures on a class hated for their abominations, called Christians by the populace" (*Annals* 15.44).

Christianity was in disrepute at the time of the fire—either through deliberate slander or misunderstanding—and provided Nero with the perfect scapegoat for his own actions. Against the Christians in Rome he fanned into intense flame the fires of persecution.

Paul was caught in that new conflagration—that's why he was in prison when he wrote his second letter to Timothy. Timothy knew that if persecution spread throughout the empire he—as Paul's friend and a leader of a Christian church—might receive the same treatment Paul received. Paul wanted Timothy to be willing to suffer too. He wanted Timothy to consider suffering for Christ as much an honor as he did.

Lesson

In 2 Timothy 2:9 the phrase "for which I suffer hardship" means Paul was willing to endure evil treatment for specific reasons. In verses 8-13 Paul states four reasons that make hardship for the sake of proclaiming the gospel worth enduring.

I. THE PREEMINENCE OF CHRIST (v. 8)

"Remember Jesus Christ, risen from the dead, descendant of David, according to my gospel."

Verse 8 focuses on the preeminence of Christ—the driving motivation of Paul's ministry. "Remember" (Gk., *mnēmoneuō*) could be translated "keep always in your memory." We would serve more boldly and courageously if we never lost sight of whom we are serving.

To Paul ministry meant "serving the Lord with all humility and with tears and with trials" (Acts 20:19). He endured the tremendous obstacles put in his path because he never lost sight of whom he served—not the church, a program, or his personal ambitions but the Lord Jesus Christ. Paul understood his service to be like that of a teacher, soldier, athlete, and farmer (2 Tim. 2:2-6), looking to our Lord as his preeminent example of self-sacrifice.

First John 2:6 says, "The one who says he abides in Him ought himself to walk in the same manner as [Jesus] walked." Just as He was for Paul, the Lord is our example also.

A. His Deity

The phrase "Jesus Christ, risen from the dead" (2 Tim. 2:8) is literally translated "Jesus Christ, risen out from among the dead." The resurrection of Christ was selective—Paul calls Him the "first-born" or "preeminent one" (Gk., *prōtotokos*) from among the dead (Col. 1:18). Paul's point in both 2 Timothy and Colossians is that Christ is preeminent and living. Because of those two ongoing realities we are to keep Him in constant memory as He is *now*.

The resurrection pictures God's destruction of death, which is Satan's greatest weapon. It also pictures salvation. Christ's death was a death for sin. His being alive means the penalty for sin is satisfied. The resurrection points to the living Christ who is both God and Savior.

B. His Humanity and Royalty

Christ is a "descendant of David" (2 Tim. 2:8). The Greek text says He is out of the *spermatos* of David. Christ was from the loins of David, which presents Him both as a man and a royal heir. We are to be motivated in our service by remembering that the one we serve is the God-man/Savior-King.

C. His Suffering

Our Lord suffered before He was glorified, was humiliated before He was crowned, and died before His resurrection. Since that's the path to glory the perfect Son of God followed, we should expect to walk it too, for we are no better than our Savior.

Hebrews 5:8 says, "Although [Christ] was a Son, He learned obedience from the things which He suffered." Christians should expect to learn obedience in the same way. That's contrary to today's prosperity gospel, which teaches that God desires only happiness for His children in this world. It's also contrary to what the Bible says about repentance (a message not warmly received in our society). We must be willing to suffer with Christ and tell others they will suffer for Christ if they enter a saving relationship with Him.

D. His Example

Our Lord is the supreme example of how all Christians are to react to suffering. First Peter 2:21-23 says, "You have been called for this purpose [patient suffering], since Christ also suffered for you, leaving you an example for you to follow in His steps, who committed no sin, nor was any deceit found in His mouth; and while being reviled, He did not revile in return; while suffering, He uttered no threats, but kept entrusting Himself to Him who judges righteously." We are to react to suffering in the same way our Lord did.

Christ endured suffering for the sake of the truth. Hebrews 12:2 says that "for the joy set before Him endured the cross, despising the shame, and has sat down at the right hand of the throne of God." Our Lord was willing to patiently endure the shame of the cross because He saw the glory to come. As we live for Him with boldness and courage, suffering as we do so, we are to remember our Savior and follow His example. We may do so confident of the glory to come.

E. His Resurrection

When we remember our Lord we must remember that He lives! He reigns now at the right hand of the Father in heaven as the royal heir of David. He lives to intercede as our great High Priest and reigns as sovereign over all creation. That realization ought to affect how we respond to the hatred of men toward Christ and us. He who suffered remembers our suffering and will bring us to glory.

F. His Worthy Cause

To remember Jesus is to remember He is the *prōtotokos* (Col. 1:8)—the preeminent one. The worthiness of Christ's Person makes His cause worthy—a cause worth giving one's life for.

If we remember that Jesus Christ is the God-man, Savior-King, faithful High Priest, and sovereign over all creation with the most worthy cause of any, we will happily give our lives for that cause. I am amazed to see pagan monks setting themselves on fire for demonic causes whereas many professing Christians refuse to give themselves for the preeminent cause of Christ—a cause fully worth living and dying for.

A well-trained memory forgets all that's not worth remembering and remembers all that is important. The only thing worth remembering is Jesus Christ and living for Him.

II. THE POWER OF THE WORD (v. 9)

"I suffer hardship even to imprisonment as a criminal; but the word of God is not imprisoned."

A. The Bound Messenger

The King James Version of 2 Timothy 2:9 declares that "the word of God is not bound." That's the reason Paul could write with confidence in the midst of evil treatment and imprisonment. Though he was imprisoned, the Word of God was free.

1. Paul's imprisonment

The Greek word translated "imprisonment" can refer to a prisoner's chains (e.g., 2 Tim. 1:16), but "criminal" implies something more: Paul was considered a criminal and treated like one. At the time Paul wrote 2 Timothy he was in the Mamertine prison in Rome. It was a pit without normal sanitation jammed with people awaiting execution. Undoubtedly they were not comfortable with Paul's presence, nor was he with theirs. This was a much rougher situation than the house arrest of his first imprisonment in Rome (cf. Acts 28:16-31). Paul's use of the word translated "criminal" (Gk., *kakourgos*, a technical word used of robbers, such as those crucified with Jesus) may reflect the shame Paul felt by being classified by the Roman government in the same way as those he was incarcerated with.

2. Paul's critics

Paul's sense of shame may have been increased by those who were glad he had been imprisoned. They might have said to him, "Why did you keep preaching and get yourself thrown into prison? You should have softened your message and stopped attacking public figures. Why couldn't you have quietly passed out tracts and left before people knew you were here? You weren't subtle—now your ministry is a mess!" Such criticisms would have weighed heavily on Paul's heart.

Politics and the Gospel

Today some think the only reason we can freely share the gospel in America is because America is free. So they spend large

42

amounts of time in political action to maintain a free America. Certainly a free America means the freedom to preach the gospel—but the gospel is unbound regardless of America's political system.

Paul affirmed that even though he was imprisoned, the gospel could never be imprisoned. That's an important message for those who say we need to soften the gospel message so we don't lose the freedom to preach it. They say we need to take away the offense of the gospel, but that would rob the gospel of its power (cf. 1 Cor. 1:23-25).

Some will respond, "If we boldly proclaim an offensive gospel we may be arrested and jailed." But if that's where the Lord wants us to be, then that's great! Paul wrote to the Philippians, "All the saints greet you, especially [the new believers] of Caesar's household" (Phil. 4:22). Paul was a prisoner when he wrote that, yet many in Caesar's household had come to faith in Christ through his witness in such circumstances. Paul viewed imprisonment as an opportunity to evangelize his guards (cf. Phil. 1:12-13).

In 2 Timothy 4:2 he says, "Preach the word; be ready in season and out of season; reprove, rebuke, exhort, with great patience and instruction." That's a call to preach boldly without compromising the message of the gospel—even if it means chains and death. Paul could write that with assurance because he knew he proclaimed a gospel with power.

B. The Unbound Message

1. The testimony of Martin Luther

In his hymn "A Mighty Fortress Is Our God" Martin Luther wrote, "The body they may kill: God's truth abideth still." Luther knew that regardless of what happens to us, God's Word remains unbound.

2. The testimony of the early church

During the persecution the church endured in its early years, many Christians hid in caverns in Rome and outlying areas. They dug many miles of catacombs and buried their dead there for nearly three hundred years. Archaeologists estimate that as many as four million Christians were buried in those catacombs. When I visited the remains of those catacombs, I saw the inscription "The Word of God is not bound." Those persecuted Christians knew that even though they might be killed, no one could stop the Word of God.

3. The testimony of John Bunyan

When John Bunyan, the author of *The Pilgrim's Progress*, was imprisoned in Bedford jail, his cell was in a building inside a high wall. During the day crowds would gather outside the wall and listen to Bunyan as he preached. His voice carried over the wall through the bars of his cell widow. The Word of God was not bound.

4. The testimony of the church in China

Countless numbers of Christians died for their faith when the Communists took over China. Ever since then the church has been persecuted and oppressed. Yet it is estimated that it has grown to between 30 and 100 million believers. That couldn't have happened if the power of the Word depended on political conditions.

In his book *The Church in China* Carl Lawrence says that in the house churches of China "sometimes the absence of those who are not there is as significant as the presence of those who are.

"Missing from the meetings is a young science teacher, a Christian who refused to teach Darwin's theory of evolution as truth. She told officials that Darwin was anti-God and that the theory of evolution was not true. For weeks they tried to persuade her. Good science teachers were difficult to find, especially after the Cultural Revolution. She would not relent. Her reply was always the same. 'We are not monkeys. We are men and women made in the image of God.' Later she would cry the same words through broken teeth and bloody lips.

"Today, she is a janitor at the school and is forbidden to attend house meetings with her fellow believers.

"There is also the noticeable void left by the beloved doctor who refused to confess that Chairman Mao was bigger than 'your Christ.'

"He was beaten and left unconscious by the Red Guard. They covered him with a blanket and let him lie on the hospital floor. They told him they would be back in a few days. They returned and his response was simple, 'My Christ is bigger than Chairman Mao. My Christ is the Lord of lords, King of kings. He has been given the name above all names in heaven, on earth and under the earth.'

"More beating, but the same response: 'My Christ is bigger.' After several days, they decided to end this heresy once and for all. They stripped him naked and made him stand up on a narrow bench, barely six inches wide. 'Now,' they shouted, 'if your Christ is bigger than Chairman Mao, let Him save you! Our Chairman Mao can save you; just admit it.'

"Quietly and barely audible, he repeated the story of the men in the fiery furnace. He raised his voice as he looked at his persecutors and told them, 'They were not burned because the Lord stood with them, and He is with me now.'

"The hours passed, not a muscle in his body trembled. Five hours, ten hours—people began to take notice. 'Where does this old man get his strength?' they asked. His very presence was becoming, not only a witness to Christ, but a source of conviction and embarrassment to the others who saw him standing, naked, on the bench.

"Finally, the cadre could stand it no longer. Naked, and without a whimper, the 'man who believed Christ bigger than Chairman Mao' had stood, balancing himself on a narrow bench, from seven in the evening until ten the next morning. After fifteen hours of what he called 'peace and fellowship,' he was pushed to the floor. The Red Guard promised him that there would be another day. It came a week later. Dragging him away from his patients, they hanged him.

"The Red Guard fought among themselves. They were frightened. Some wanted to cut him down before he died. After a scuffle, one cut the rope. He fell to the floor and preached his last message: 'As I was hanging there, my heart was melting for you.' He then died, as his predecessor, Stephen, had done before him" ([Minneapolis: Bethany, 1985], pp. 42-43; used by permission).

That kind of persecution has not killed off the church in China, even though Bibles are scarce: "In 1966, the Red Guards made a concentrated effort to burn all the Bibles, hymnals and other Christian literature. They did their job well. Today, it is not uncommon to see a group of several hundred people with only one Bible" (Lawrence, pp. 61-62). One witness of the situation in China said, "I know of one village where there are 5,000 believers and four preachers, but not one complete Bible. One person has a New Testament which begins with the thirteenth chapter of Mark and goes through the book of Titus" (p. 62). Another says, "I have 3,000 people in the house churches that I visit and teach. We have three complete Bibles and two New Testaments" (pp. 66-67).

The writer of Hebrews wrote that "the word of God is living and active and sharper than any two-edged sword" (Heb. 4:12). It can't be bound—that's why we can preach it with confidence and without fear of the consequences.

Conclusion

We shouldn't fear to preach the truth of Christ boldly. Christians in America need to catch fire spiritually and begin to preach biblical truth boldly and without compromise. That might result in hostility toward us—but perhaps that hostility would be used by God to purify the church in America. Christians

46

need to covenant together to remember Christ and that His Word can't be bound.

Focusing on the Facts

1. Second Timothy 2:8-13 gives _____ for sacrificial service that all Christians can learn from (see p. 36).
2. Show from Scripture that to confess Jesus as Lord means to submit to Him and serve His cause (see p. 36).
3. How extreme may the sacrifice be that a Christian is called on to make for the Lord (see p. 37)?
4. How do we know that the Word of God and a godly life will create conflict with the world (2 Tim. 3:12; see p. 37)?
5. What result did the burning of Rome have on the Christian community? What was its impact on Paul (see pp. 37-38)?
6. What does 2 Timothy 2:8 focus on (see p. 39)?
7. What did ministry mean to Paul (Acts 20:19; see p. 39)?
8. Paul's point in both 2 Timothy 2:8 and Colossians 1:18 is that Christ is _____ and _____ (see p. 39).
9. What does the resurrection picture (see p. 39)?
10. How does the description of Christ as a "descendant of David" (2 Tim. 2:8) present Him to us (see p. 40)?
11. Since the path to glory the perfect Son of God followed was one of suffering, what should we expect? What is that message contrary to? What does that indicate we must tell others if they consider entering a saving relationship with Christ (see p. 40)?
12. Our Lord is the supreme _____ of how all Christians are to react to suffering (see p. 40).
13. Why was our Lord willing to patiently endure the shame of the cross (Heb. 12:2; see pp. 40-41)?
14. Why was Paul able to write Timothy with confidence in the midst of evil treatment and imprisonment (see p. 42)?
15. How did Paul's second imprisonment in Rome differ from his first (see p. 42)?
16. Second Timothy 2:9 says that the Word of God is not bound. Discuss how history has borne that out (see pp. 42-46).

Pondering the Principles

1. Nineteenth-century English pastor Charles Haddon Spurgeon said, "Oh, what mercy is that which has turned our hell to heaven, transformed our disease into health, and lifted us from the dunghill, and set us among the princes of His people! In infinite power to remove sin, to perfume with acceptance, to clothe with righteousness, to win blessings, to preserve saints, and to save to the uttermost, the Lord Jesus is great beyond all greatness" (*The Treasury of the Bible*, vol. 1 [Grand Rapids: Zondervan, 1962], p. 606). Powerful ministry for Christ depends on your mind-set. When you "remember Jesus Christ" (2 Tim. 2:8) is it with a mind-set that affirms He is "great beyond all greatness"?

2. Whereas God's Word is unbound, the hearts of those who truly know God's Word are to be bound by its teaching. Yet the watching world must often wonder what power—if any—God's Word has when it looks at those who profess to know the God of the Bible. A. W. Tozer said, "The difficulty we modern Christians face is not misunderstanding the Bible, but persuading our untamed hearts to accept its plain instructions" (cited in *Signposts: A Collection of Sayings from A. W. Tozer*, Harry Verploegh, ed. [Wheaton, Ill.: Victor, 1988], p. 16). When the unsaved examine your life do they see a heart bound by God's Word and a life governed by it?

4

Motives for Sacrificial Ministry— Part 2

Outline

Introduction
A. An Old Testament Precedent
   1. Jeremiah's predicament
   2. God's answer
B. The New Testament Pattern

Review
  I. The Preeminence of Christ (v. 8)
  II. The Power of the Word (v. 9)

Lesson
  III. The Purpose of the Work (v. 10)
    A. Why We Are to Suffer
    B. How We Are to Suffer
      1. The example of John Wesley
      2. The example of George Whitefield
  IV. The Promised Reward (vv. 11-13)
    A. The Positive Reward
      1. Life through death
      2. Reigning through endurance
    B. The Negative Reward
      1. Denial for denial
      2. Faithfulness for faithlessness

Conclusion

Introduction

When the apostle Paul wrote 2 Timothy, the namesake of his letter had apparently reached a low point in his spiritual life and ministry. Because of the difficulties he was facing, Timothy may have developed an attitude of self-pity. Paul did not respond with sympathy but with an exhortation to spiritual strength. The appropriateness of that response can be seen elsewhere in Scripture.

A. An Old Testament Precedent

1. Jeremiah's predicament

The prophet Jeremiah was the epitome of righteousness and godliness in his day. He did not live a happy life and would have been a poor advertisement for today's prosperity gospel. He was born a priest but exercised the office of a prophet. He endured extreme suffering for most of his life, which was an ongoing martyrdom. The people of Israel hated him so much that, had God not spared him, he would have been killed on numerous occasions.

During the years of Jeremiah's ministry the people of Israel were apostate. God called him to deliver a confronting message of repentance and holiness that the people did not want to hear. At times he felt God had abandoned him—he even cursed the day he was born (Jer. 20:14).

King Jehoiakim once became so angry with Jeremiah that he cut the scroll of Jeremiah's prophecy into pieces and burned it (36:20-26). King Zedekiah imprisoned him. He endured more opposition than any other Old Testament prophet.

Much of the opposition to Jeremiah was due to his uncompromising message of total commitment to God. Tradition says that he was stoned to death because of his message. Yet in the midst of such rejection Jeremiah wept at the prospect of the coming judgment God would bring upon his people (9:1).

Jeremiah 11:21 records one of the many sorrows in the life of Jeremiah: the men of his home village of Anathoth sought to kill him. They threatened him, saying, "Do not prophesy in the name of the Lord, that you might not die at our hand." They were angry because of the condemning prophecies Jeremiah had uttered against Israel.

In response to that threat Jeremiah turned to God for an answer: "Righteous art Thou, O Lord, that I would plead my case with Thee; indeed I would discuss matters of justice with Thee: Why has the way of the wicked prospered? Why are all those who deal in treachery at ease?" (12:1). He didn't consider his predicament to be fair and said to God, "Thou knowest me, O Lord; Thou seest me; and Thou dost examine my heart's attitude toward Thee" (v. 3). It appeared to him that God was prospering the wicked (v. 2) while he—a righteous and true servant of God—was allowed to suffer. He wanted to know how long the land was "to mourn and the vegetation of the countryside to wither" (v. 4). He wanted to know how God could allow the wicked to prosper while the righteous were persecuted.

Jeremiah's questions to God have been asked by many suffering saints. I have struggled with the prosperity of others while I was persecuted for preaching the truth—and my difficulties have been nothing like what Jeremiah suffered! Yet it's natural for God's servants to cry out to Him when suffering comes, wondering how their pain can be reconciled with God's justice.

2. God's answer

God's answer to Jeremiah is striking—He didn't offer sympathy or consolation. Jeremiah asked God to punish his enemies (v. 3), but instead God told Jeremiah, "If you have run with footmen and they have tired you out, then how can you compete with horses? If you fall down in a land of peace, how will you do in the thicket of the Jordan?" (v. 5). In effect God was saying, "You may think you've suffered up to now, but you haven't even begun to suffer." Jeremiah had been running against mere men, but soon he would be running against horses—a much tougher race. Jeremiah's present suffering was like being in a land of peace compared to the future, which would be like a wild jungle.

Jeremiah's present sufferings were but training for suffering to come. God's answer to Jeremiah was not a show of sympathy but a call to spiritual strength.

B. The New Testament Pattern

God's response to Jeremiah's cry for help was the same response Paul made to Timothy's lack of resolve in the face of persecution. God warned Jeremiah that he needed resolve as he faced treacherous dealing by those closest to him (Jer. 12:6). Paul exhorted Timothy to spiritual strength in light of actual and anticipated persecution (2 Tim. 2:1-7). In 2 Timothy 2:8-13 Paul undergirds that exhortation with motivations for Timothy to fulfill his calling—motivations that apply to us as well.

We find similar motivation in Hebrews 12:3, which says, "Consider Him who has endured such hostility by sinners against Himself, so that you may not grow weary and lose heart." Jesus affirmed that, like Him, His disciples would suffer persecution: "A disciple is not above his teacher, nor a slave above his master. It is enough for the disciple that he become as his teacher, and the slave as his master. If they have called the head of the house Beelzebul, how much more the members of his household!" (Matt. 10:24-25). That's a warning we need to remember.

Three times in Matthew 10 Jesus exhorts His followers not to fear persecution (vv. 26, 28, 31). We are not to fear because God knows about our circumstances, cares for us, oversees us, and will vindicate us in the end. In light of such assurances we are called to sacrifice all that hinders our relationship to Christ (cf. Matt. 10:34-37; Heb. 12:1-2). Christ promises that "he who has found his life shall lose it, and he who has lost his life for My sake shall find it" (Matt. 10:39).

Hebrews 11 describes saints who were willing to endure persecution, commenting that the world was not worthy of them (v. 38). They devoted themselves to God's will because they had a higher agenda than the things of this world. That's the agenda Paul calls us to in 2 Timothy. It's an agenda we can meet only if we are motivated by more than our own desire for personal well-being. If comfort, prosperity, success, and fame motivate you, you will not be able to endure persecution for Christ's sake. The church has been built on those motivated by a Christlike agenda.

Review

Believers have four truths to motivate them in the face of persecution. Second Timothy 2:8-13 says, "Remember Jesus Christ, risen from the dead, descendant of David, according to my gospel, for which I suffer hardship even to imprisonment as a criminal; but the word of God is not imprisoned. For this reason I endure all things for the sake of those who are chosen, that they also may obtain the salvation which is in Christ Jesus and with it eternal glory. It is a trustworthy statement: For if we died with Him, we shall also live with Him; if we endure, we shall also reign with Him; if we deny Him, He also will deny us; if we are faithless, He remains faithful; for He cannot deny Himself."

I. THE PREEMINENCE OF CHRIST (v. 8; see pp. 39-41)

If you're focused on yourself, you won't tell others about Christ. You will compromise to avoid offending people. You won't confront evil with righteousness. In family situations you won't confront spiritual error with the truth. People who endure without compromising are like Daniel: they are willing to endure a lions' den rather than compromise their relationship with the preeminent Christ.

II. THE POWER OF THE WORD (v. 9; see pp. 41-46)

Lesson

III. THE PURPOSE OF THE WORK (v. 10)

"For this reason I endure all things for the sake of those who are chosen, that they also may obtain the salvation which is in Christ Jesus and with it eternal glory."

A. Why We Are to Suffer

The phrase "for this reason" (v. 10) explains Paul's willingness to work and endure suffering. He was willing to suffer "all things" (hardship, sacrifice, persecution, chains, and prison) "for the sake of those who are chosen"—the elect.

Scripture identifies some people as elect—chosen by God for salvation from the foundation of the world (Eph. 1:4). Some might ask, "If those people are elect, won't God save them regardless of what they do? Why should Paul or anyone else endure suffering when they're going to be saved anyway? I sure wouldn't!"

That's an unbalanced view of the doctrine of election. Verse 10 balances it with the words "That they also may obtain the salvation which is in Christ Jesus and with it eternal glory." In that statement Paul explains that he was willing to suffer for the elect that they might obtain what they have been elected to. God not only chooses those who will be saved but also chooses believers to be the instruments for bringing His people to salvation.

A Christian isn't given spiritual life so that he can move up the corporate ladder, make more money, buy a new camper, go on a longer vacation, get new furniture for the living room, or buy a new house. Every Christian's foremost desire should be to be used by God for evangelizing and edifying God's elect. Whereas from God's perspective salvation is by God's choice, from man's perspective it is obtained by faith. That's accomplished in time as God uses believers to proclaim the gospel, bringing the elect into a saving relationship with Christ.

54

Romans 10:13-15 says, "'Whoever will call upon the name of the Lord will be saved.' How then shall they call upon Him in whom they have not believed? And how shall they believe in Him whom they have not heard? And how shall they hear without a preacher? And how shall they preach unless they are sent? Just as it is written, 'How beautiful are the feet of those who bring glad tidings of good things!'" We are called to preach the gospel so that the elect may call upon the name of the Lord and be saved. Paul was willing to endure anything to fulfill that calling.

B. How We Are to Suffer

1. The example of John Wesley

John Wesley parted company with ease early in his ministry. He lived simply, giving away nearly all he had for the advance of the gospel. He was abused and maligned in his day but resolved to leave his reputation in the hands of God. He is said to have traveled 225,000 miles by foot or horseback and preached 2,400 sermons, all the while under attack by mobs, other preachers, and the press. He was misrepresented and did not know the comforts of home, yet he never lost the joy of the ministry. His mind was set on Whom he was serving, not the things of the world.

2. The example of George Whitefield

George Whitefield was greatly used by God in America after being used in England. In thirty-four years he crossed the Atlantic Ocean thirteen times and preached thousands of sermons. It is said that as a soldier of the cross, humble, ardent, devout, he put on the whole armor of God, preferring the honor of Christ to his own interest, repose, reputation, or life.

Why should we be willing to follow the example of others and endure suffering for the sake of Christ's elect? Because we have the privilege of participating in a marvelous work. Those who avoid proclaiming the gospel for fear of offense lose that privilege, and God gives it to others who will obey Him. In Acts 18:9-10 the Lord tells the apostle Paul, "Do not

55

be afraid any longer, but go on speaking and do not be silent; for I am with you, and no man will attack you in order to harm you, for I have many people in this city." Paul obeyed, and we are to do the same.

IV.   THE PROMISED REWARD (vv. 11-13)

"It is a trustworthy statement: For if we died with Him, we shall also live with Him; if we endure, we shall also reign with Him; if we deny Him, He also will deny us; if we are faithless, He remains faithful; for He cannot deny Himself."

Verses 11-13 make one of five faithful, or trustworthy, sayings in the pastoral epistles of Paul (cf. 1 Tim. 1:15; 3:1; 4:9-10; 2 Tim. 2:11-13; Titus 3:4-8). They were sayings that expressed axiomatic ideas in the early church—truisms everyone knew to be accurate reflections of the gospel. Because of the parallelism and rhythmic structure, verses 11-13 may be a hymn sung by the early church.

A. The Positive Reward

When Paul wrote 2 Timothy the church was under increasing persecution. Therefore it must have been of great comfort to be able to affirm that "if we died with Him, we shall also live with Him" (v. 11).

1. Life through death

Verses 11-13 are stated as first-class conditions in the Greek text; each "if" can be read as expressing reality —not merely a possibility. In verse 11 "we died" is expressed in the Greek text as an aorist-tense verb, which views the action of the verb as a completed whole, whereas "we will" is in the future tense. Thus verse 11 could be translated, "If at any time we have died with Him, we will in the future live with Him."

The presence of aorist and future tenses in verse 11 shows the effect of a present reality on the future. Verse 11 promises that loss of life in the present means the gain of life in the future. That reality is implicit in Paul's statement "To be absent from the body [is] to be at home with the Lord" (2 Cor. 5:8).

Similarly Jesus looked forward to spiritual life beyond death as an absolute certainty, as did the martyred Stephen (cf. Luke 23:46; Acts 7:59).

Verse 11 may also carry the implication that those who have died in Christ by faith now live and walk in newness of life (cf. Rom. 6:2-4). But the main purpose of Paul's statement here is to assure those who face martyrdom that death for Christ's sake will certainly result in spiritual life in His presence.

2. Reigning through endurance

In verse 12 Paul moves from martyrdom to present endurance. The verb translated "endure" speaks of continual, patient, present endurance. Most of us won't be martyrs, but we all need to patiently endure whatever suffering and persecution we experience. The promise for such endurance is that "we shall also reign with [Christ]" (v. 12), entering into His presence immediately upon death.

Death or endurance for Christ's cause will be worth bearing in light of coming glory. We may have to submit to persecution, animosity, and bitterness now, but the future holds life, authority, and exaltation in the presence of Christ for all who are loyal to Him. We will live and reign (Gk., *sumbasileuō*, "to reign together with") with Christ. Those are wonderful promises!

The Perseverance of the Saints

The promises in 2 Timothy 2:11-12 speak not only of faithful service to Christ but also of the perseverance of the saints. All genuine Christians stay true to their Savior through whatever trials, struggles, persecutions, and difficulties they may pass. That's not to say there won't be momentary lapses, but true Christians who lapse eventually repent of their sin and go on to persevere in life. Though Peter denied his Lord, he repented and wept bitterly (Mark 14:66-72). Tradition says that Peter died a martyr's death, just as His Lord predicted (cf. John 21:18).

Everyone else who is elect likewise perseveres. We are secure in our salvation by God's choice and made to be secure by His power. Those who persevere demonstrate that God is indeed at work in them unto salvation (Phil. 2:12-13).

In John 8:31 Jesus says to "those Jews who had believed Him, 'If you abide in My word, then you are truly disciples of Mine.'" In 1 Corinthians 15:1-2 Paul reminds the Corinthians of "the gospel which I preached to you, which also you received, in which also you stand, by which also you are saved, *if you hold fast the word which I preached to you*, unless you believed in vain" (emphasis added). It's possible to profess to believe in Christ yet not be saved. Making a "decision for Christ" or "accepting Christ" mean nothing apart from perseverance. Those terms aren't even found in Scripture. In Scripture when a person is invited to salvation in Christ, it is always an invitation to follow Christ —not just to accept Christ so that He'll give you a wonderful life.

Evangelism that offers a Christ who does not demand to be followed has produced a lot of still-births—people who think they are born again but have not understood the nature of a relationship to Christ and do not show perseverance in the Christian faith. Calling people to salvation in Christ is a call to correct doctrine and a living discipleship, not to a meaningless decision void of loyalty or faithfulness to Christ. Only those who are loyal and faithful to Christ can rest in the promise of one day reigning with Him.

Christians once were "alienated and hostile in mind, engaged in evil deeds" (Col. 1:21). But now we are reconciled through Christ "if indeed [we] continue in the faith firmly established and steadfast, and not moved away from the hope of the gospel that [we] have heard" (v. 23). That means we must be faithful followers if we are to look forward to reigning with Christ.

B. The Negative Reward

The hymn in 2 Timothy 2:11-13 also has a negative side. Verses 12-13 declare, "If we endure, we shall also reign with Him; if we deny Him, He also will deny us; if we are faithless, He remains faithful; for He cannot deny Himself."

1. Denial for denial

The Greek verb translated "deny" means "to reject," "disown," or "renounce" (cf. Acts 3:13; Titus 1:16; 2 Pet. 2:1). It is stated in the future tense, implying that some who call themselves Christians will deny Christ in the future. The promise to such people is that Christ will likewise deny them.

They are like the rocky soil described in Mark 4, for "when they hear the word, [they] immediately receive it with joy; and they have no firm root in themselves, but are only temporary; then, when affliction or persecution arises because of the word, immediately they fall away" (vv. 16-17). That refers not to someone who temporarily denies Christ but to one who continually disowns and renounces Christ without repentance.

The promise in 2 Timothy 2:12 was stated by Christ Himself: "Everyone . . . who shall confess Me before men, I will also confess him before My Father who is in heaven. But whoever shall deny Me before men, I will also deny him before My Father who is in heaven" (Matt. 10:32-33). Those who deny Christ are the Demases of the world: they love "this present world" (2 Tim. 4:10). They will follow Jesus for a while, but when a difficulty arises they will leave Him (cf. John 6:60-66). They are those to whom Jesus will say on the day of judgment, "I never knew you; depart from Me, you who practice lawlessness" (Matt. 7:23).

2. Faithfulness for faithlessness

Similar to verse 12, verse 13 warns of coming judgment for those who at one time profess to know Christ but later deny Him and become faithless. In my life I have known many such people. Many whom I grew up with once professed faith in Christ but now completely deny Christianity. They are unfaithful to their promise to Christ.

59

Christ's promise to the faithless is damnation. The Greek verb translated "we are faithless" (*apisteō*) means "not to believe" and implies a continual state of unbelief. According to John 3:18, "he who does not believe has been judged already, because he has not believed in the name of the only begotten Son of God." That is God's promise, and God is faithful to fulfill all His promises. So when Paul says that "He remains faithful; for He cannot deny Himself," he means the faithless will be judged and condemned as promised.

Second Timothy 2:11-13 is a trustworthy statement about rewards and punishments. Two positive statements promise eternal life and reigning with Christ to those who endure for Christ no matter what. Two corresponding negative statements promise Christ's denial and judgment to those who deny Him and are faithless. Therefore we ought to serve Christ and endure anything for the glorious reward He promises.

Conclusion

American President Theodore Roosevelt declared, "It is not the critic who counts; not the man who points out how the strong man stumbled or where the doer of deed could have done better. The credit belongs to the man who is actually in the arena, who's face is marred by dust and sweat and blood, who strives valiantly; who errs, and comes short again and again, because there is no effort without error and shortcoming; who does actually try to do the deed; who knows the great enthusiasm, the great devotion and spends himself in a worthy cause; who, at the worst, if he fails, at least fails while daring greatly.

"Far better is it to dare mighty things, to win glorious triumphs even though checked by failure, than to rank with those poor spirits who neither enjoy nor suffer much because they live in a gray twilight that knows little victory nor defeat" (cf. Hamilton Club speech, Chicago, 10 Apr. 1899).

We are to be loyal, faithful, consistent, sacrificial, and endur-ing—not living in the gray twilight of a life that doesn't count for God. In light of the preeminence of Christ, the power of His Word, the purpose of the work, and the promise of reward, Paul says at the beginning of 2 Timothy 2:14, "Remind them of these things." That's what Timothy was to do because of who Christ is, and that's what we're always to remember.

Focusing on the Facts

1. Why would the prophet Jeremiah have been a poor adver-tisement for today's prosperity gospel (see p. 50)?
2. It is natural for God's servants to cry out to Him whenever _____ comes (see p. 51).
3. What was God's answer to Jeremiah's predicament (see pp. 51-52)?
4. Why shouldn't Christians fear persecution (see p. 52)?
5. What kind of agenda does Paul call us to in 2 Timothy (see p. 53)?
6. For whose sake was Paul willing to suffer "all things" (2 Tim. 2:10; see p. 54)?
7. Every Christian's foremost desire should be to be used by God for _____ and _____ _____ _____ (see p. 54).
8. What was John Wesley's response when he was abused and maligned (see p. 55)?
9. What do the faithful sayings in the pastoral epistles express (see p. 56)?
10. What do the Greek tenses in verse 11 show (see p. 56)?
11. What is the main purpose of Paul's statement in verse 11 (see p. 57)?
12. What promise is given to those who endure suffering and persecution for Christ's sake (2 Tim. 2:12; see p. 57)?
13. Do believers experience lapses in their endurance? If so, do such lapses become ongoing (see p. 57)?
14. Is it possible to profess belief in Christ yet not be saved? Explain (see p. 58).
15. Describe those who deny Christ (Mark 4:16-17; see p. 59).
16. What is Christ's promise to the faithless (2 Tim. 2:13; see p. 60)?

Pondering the Principles

1. J. C. Ryle said of George Whitefield, "He was a man of remarkable disinterestedness and singleness of eye. He seemed to live only for two objects—the glory of God and the salvation of souls. Of secondary and covert objects he knew nothing at all. He established no denominational system, of which his own writings should be cardinal elements. A favourite expression of his is most characteristic of the man: 'Let the name of George Whitefield perish, so long as Christ is exalted'" (*Christian Leaders of the 18th Century* [Edinburgh: Banner of Truth Trust, p. 58). Only a mind fixed firmly on the glory of Christ alone can endure whatever comes so that God's elect might be called and saved. A mind fixed on other things inevitably falters. If you hope to endure and lead others to Christ, ask yourself this: *On what is my mind set?*

2. Jeremiah wrote the book of Lamentations after the fall and destruction of Jerusalem in 586 B.C. In spite of the devastation, the "weeping prophet" remarkably declared, "The Lord's lovingkindnesses indeed never cease, for His compassions never fail. They are new every morning; great is Thy faithfulness" (3:22-23). Jeremiah worshiped and proclaimed a God who is faithful to Himself and His Word. The destruction of Jerusalem proved God's faithfulness to judge the ungodly (Jer. 4:4-9; Hab. 1:5-11), yet Jeremiah had already prophesied that God in faithfulness to His promise to Israel would restore His people (Jer. 29:10). God is indeed faithful to do what He has promised in His Word. If you are a follower of Jesus Christ, take comfort in God's promise that none who belong to Christ will be lost and all will enjoy eternal life and exaltation with Him (John 6:39). If you refuse to follow Christ, God has promised to judge you with His eternal wrath (John 3:18, 36). Turn to Christ now, and exchange the promise of judgment for that of exaltation in the presence of God!

Scripture Index

Topical Index